From Valet to Millionaire

10 Secrets To Become A Millionaire "They" Don't Tell You

By Austin Rutherford

This book is dedicated to my family; Mom, Dad, Grandmother, and my sister. Thank you for supporting me in all of my endeavors and never holding me back!

Table of Contents

Forward, By Mark Evans

When I told my family I was never going to work for someone, they all told me I was crazy. There's nothing wrong with the hard-working blue-collar jobs my parents held... I just wanted something else for my life.

When I bought my first company at the age of eighteen, a small company from a guy who wanted to retire, people were shocked. They didn't think what I did was even possible since I didn't come from money, and the fact that most kids the same age were working weekends at a gas station.

When I nearly burnt out and went bankrupt, people were shocked that I kept going. I was determined to figure it out instead of shutting it down. (Hint: I did figure it out!)

When I moved to South Beach, Florida to run my business virtually—essentially building a team to do the work for me while

I directed them from the beach—people were shocked again. They didn't think you could run a business that way.

When I started traveling the world with my then-fiancé (now my wife), Deena, while my businesses ran themselves, people were shocked *yet again*. They didn't think someone could run a business that way. And I did it for 7 years.

Today I run several 7- and 8-figure businesses while I spend time with my wife and son, Mark III, (and one child on the way) in Florida, Ohio, or anywhere we choose. Not surprisingly, people are still shocked and never shy to tell me that a CEO of several large organizations should be wearing a suit and working in an office.

I don't tell you any of this to impress you, but to impress upon you that the thoughts and opinions of others don't matter as much as your ability to roll up your sleeve and build the life and business you want.

If I'd listened to everyone else, I'd be living an average life; that's not what I wanted. I've always been a little different that way and have never felt the need to apologize for it. And when I met Austin Rutherford three years ago, I saw in him the same thing I have felt in my own life…

The first time I met Austin was at an event I was speaking at. He approached me, based in part on the recommendation of a mutual friend who said that we needed to meet.

From the moment we met, I knew that Austin was different— in a good way!

Over the years, I've met many people who want to take over the world… who have an idea that they are sure will be a winner, or who want to achieve some form of "business success" (whatever that means) so they can have the toys and lifestyle.

But as someone who has enjoyed building a life that seems to confound the expectations of other people, I can tell you that there are MANY who WANT to take over the world but very FEW who actually CAN.

Truthfully, many lack the hustle and hard work required; and, many more can't get over shocking other people (as I have) to achieve the life they want. Too many people have dreams but aren't willing to break past their comfort zones and the opinions of others to get what they want.

Austin is different. Like all successful folks I know, he sets big goals and willingly puts in the work to achieve them. He'd already achieved a lot when he came to me and I've had the privilege to be a mentor to him when he joined The DM Family (a group I run of high-level entrepreneurs). It's not only my privilege to mentor Austin; it's also a privilege to call him my friend.

Since we've met, he's done even more... he's brought a level of hustle to his life and business that few will ever understand, and he's moving closer to his MASSIVE goals. Austin has accomplished a lot at a young age but what I know to be true is Austin is just getting started and hasn't scratched the surface of where he's going. It's a privilege to watch him and guide him.

When he showed me a draft of the book he was writing and asked me to write the foreword, I told him it would be my honor. This book is a powerful resource for anyone who wants to work hard to achieve their goals in life. He writes with an actionable focus that should make this book simple to implement if you just follow the steps. (Hint: you'll want to read this book more than once.)

Read the book. Read it again. Learn and apply. Work toward your business goals. And when you meet Austin to thank him, tell him "The DM" sent you.

I'm proud of you, Austin. Keep doing you!

Mark Evans DM

Introduction

Have you ever wanted to change the direction of your life, but don't know where to start? I'm talking about that burning desire deep inside of you, where you have literally cried or been to dark places because you think you're not living the life you are destined to live! There may be a lot of things that are holding you back from jumping in and changing your life; not enough time, no money, being sacred of the unknown, the fear of failure, friends or family telling you that you can't do it, etc.

This book will put a lot of those excuses to shame. At the end of the day, only you control your life and what you want to do with it. You can make it wildly successful and do things that most people can only dream of, or you can choose to live a mediocre life. It is going to take a lot of effort and energy to change your life, but in a short time, you will be living the life you were destined for – something other people can only dream of.

You have to be willing to get outside your comfort zone and be prepared to fail, but by doing so you will change your life very quickly!

I live each day by words that I heard years ago,

"There is only one thing in this world you can never have more of...TIME. Once it's gone, it's gone. Time doesn't wait for anyone, no matter what is happening. You can always get more of other things, but you can't get more TIME"

Sacrifice your time now so you can build something that will change your life forever! Live the life you were destined to live so that you can send your parents on vacations they would never dream of, take your family anywhere in the world, and be able to mentor other people as they change their lives.

You control your destiny! I bet on myself every time because I know I will outwork anyone else. I remember when I was younger, my dad told me, "You need to take a day off or you are going to hurt your knees," and I replied, "I don't need my knees if I don't achieve my dream of playing in the NBA." Low and behold, I didn't make the NBA, but it shows the determination and willingness I have to do whatever it takes to get to where I want to be.

I didn't make the NBA, but I found another love: real estate. It has, in less than five years, made me millions of dollars! I am going to share with you the lessons and takeaways that I have learned along the way, and if you make some slight adjustments to your thought process, you can do the same! This book will shut down any of the limiting beliefs you have as to why you shouldn't be successful, how you weren't born for it, or how to beat the fear of taking that jump into the unknown and following your dreams. I promise you that the leap of faith to follow your dreams is worth it every single time!

Chapter 1 – Get Comfortable Being Uncomfortable

When following your dreams, the first thing you are going to need to do is to get it into your head that you are going to have to get comfortable with being uncomfortable. Yes, I know that sounds crazy and the first time I heard it, I thought, "Are you mad?" However, it all makes sense now.

Maybe you are living a life where you just do the same thing every day, wake up, go to work or school, then come home to eat dinner and watch some TV, then you do it all over again the next day.

Maybe you are already chasing your dreams, going to seminars, but you're the one at the back of the room, not talking to anyone because you are scared and uncomfortable. You start to sweat just thinking about talking to someone and you freak yourself out and leave and walk away from your dreams. That was me!

The only way you are going to grow in life is by FORCING yourself out of your comfort zone. The worst thing that people can say is no, and then you will be in the same position you are in now. Just do it!

Let me tell you two stories to show you what I mean. At twenty-years-old, I was just starting my real estate business. I didn't have much money and didn't know anyone in the industry, but I had this burning desire that I wanted more out of life. I heard about a conference 2 hours away with Alan Cowgill and he was teaching people how to raise private money to fund real estate deals. I was broke at the time, so I definitely needed to raise private money to fund my dreams.

I was always on the hunt for more information and education to grow myself and my business, so even though it was a few hundred dollars to go to this event, I signed up as soon as I heard about it. However, I was young and extremely nervous, so I asked my mom to go with me to the conference. Luckily, she agreed.

Alan was teaching about raising private money and how to have conversations with private money lenders. At the end of the day, he gave us some "homework". We were to make a list of everyone that we knew who we thought could be a private money lender, and then we were to pick up the phone and call at least five of them, giving them the "pitch" and asking if they would be interested in investing with me.

When the conference finished that day, I made my list but the hard part for me was that I actually had to pick up the phone and call some of the people. I decided to start with my Uncle Steve because I was really nervous, and I figured if I got turned down by a family member it wouldn't feel as bad. I sat on the balcony of my hotel room, practicing my pitch over and over before I called my uncle. Even after I felt ready to go, I sat there for another hour, trying to get enough courage to make that first phone call. I was so scared that I would say the wrong thing and that he would say no. I thought of every possible negative outcome I could and almost didn't pick up the phone to make the call.

Finally, I called him, and he actually answered. I had been hoping that it would go to voicemail so I could at least say I made the phone call without having to deal with a no. My uncle and I chatted for a little while, then I gave him my "pitch" and he shut it down. It wasn't a hard shut down, but he basically said, "No, I can get a better investment elsewhere." My dreams were crushed. I did all of that work and preparation, yet the conversation was about five minutes long and my uncle shut me down.

What I learned, however, was priceless. First, you have to educate yourself on a topic before trying to pitch someone on it. When you know the subject, you have the confidence that you know what you are talking about and are able to answer any questions that they might have.

The second thing is to understand that the worst-case scenario is that they will say no, and you might get a little embarrassed, but you are in the same position you were just a couple minutes ago, and life goes on. Get used to the word "no". A no simply means you are one step closer to someone telling you yes. So, take each "no" as encouragement that you are moving forward.

In the past five years, I have borrowed over $15 million for my real estate projects and I have tremendous relationships with all of my private lenders, and they all trust me with their money. If I had never picked up the phone and made that first phone call, I may never have tried to raise private money from others after that. Just because you receive a no from someone, does not mean that it is a no from everyone. You just need to keep trying!

The second story I want to share with you about "making your uncomfortable comfortable" is when a mentor of mine, Mark Evans, told me that I needed to put out more content on social media (more pictures, quotes, videos, etc.). Yet, I was really scared to go on camera. I hated pictures and videos because I was just not used to doing things like that.

I was in San Diego journaling one morning when I decided I was going to do a Facebook live video. I don't even remember what the topic was on now, but I literally planned out the entire live session in my journal beforehand. I wrote down all types of notes in my journal to guide me through my time on camera. I practiced the talk and knew the flow of the conversation so it would look as if it were unscripted on camera.

I opened up the Facebook app, had my notes beside me in case I needed them, and then looked at the camera for over an hour without pressing the record button. I was so scared of the unknown, of actually putting my face on camera. I was scared of messing up, scared of what the people watching might say, and scared that nobody would even watch it.

Finally, I pressed the record button and talked. For the first minute, which felt like an eternity, nobody joined that live and I almost ended the live but I kept going and eventually people joined the live. It felt like I bombed the whole conversation as I was so nervous, stuttering over my words and looking down at my notes the whole time. Everyone must have known that this was scripted. Yet, I had good feedback from the viewers! The key takeaway here is that I did it and made myself get comfortable with being on camera.

Now, if you follow me on social media (Instagram: @AustinRutherfordOfficial Facebook: Austin Rutherford,), you will see that I am on social media all of the time, posting pictures, making IG stories, making FB stories, talking about my day or my trips or something that I learned that day. I love doing it now because I know that it is helping some people get over their own self-limiting beliefs. People that I have never talked to message me saying, "Thank you for this, it changed my life," or "This is inspiring," or "This motivates me every day to continue to follow my dreams," and that makes it all worth it. I have had people reach out to me with business opportunities because of my social media posts. I've made a lot of money from opportunities that initially came from social media. If I had never got out of my own way and recorded that first video and got comfortable with being on camera, I never would have been able to change those people's lives or make a whole stream of income from social media.

I try to force myself out of my comfort zone every day. I used to never be comfortable talking to people that I didn't know. Simply saying hello or starting a conversation with someone would make me nervous. I was scared that they would say something mean to me, or not respond and I would look "dumb". Fear of rejection even made it difficult for me to talk to women.

Everything in life, business and personal relationships, is based on conversations, and since I realized the power of speaking with people, I make a conscious effort every day to speak to anyone that comes within ten feet of me. If I am walking through the mall or am in an elevator, I speak to them and strike up a conversation. I simply say, "How are you?" It wasn't easy to start with, I was literally sweating when I would try to talk to people, but now it is so normal for me. Impromptu conversation just flows right off of my tongue. I speak to almost anyone that is even remotely close to me.

I took one of my biggest fears, talking to others, and FORCED myself out of my comfort zone every day until I was completely comfortable with what used to be really uncomfortable for me. I even created a "punishment" for myself for not approaching people that I wanted to talk to whether it was for a business opportunity, a possible mentor, or an attractive woman. If I didn't go over and speak to them and introduce myself, I had to donate $100 to a good cause. You have to make the punishment something that you really do not want to do. For me, giving $100 away every time, even if it was for a good cause, was a lot of money and something I didn't want to do. In fact, I would rather go and speak to the person than give up that money. Ironically, I have never had to donate $100 but it provided the motivation so that now I speak to people all the time – without even thinking about it!

No matter where you are in your life, you can still do anything you want to do. When you are uncomfortable, true growth happens and that is what will change your life. You can never grow in your comfort zone because you are just doing the same old stuff every single day.

If your parents are saying you need to go to college and to follow the pack, yet you don't want to and have a business plan instead, talk with them. Explain to them that just because everyone is doing it, doesn't necessarily make it the right thing or the best thing for you at this time. Maybe you are working a 9 to 5 job and that's all you know, and you are scared to do anything else... You need to get uncomfortable and try something new, like a side hustle. You have to force yourself outside your comfort zone if you ever want to grow. Start asking yourself the uncomfortable questions, going to the places where you don't know anyone, and force yourself to network, learn, and be vulnerable.

Now, you may not know what your passion is or what you really want to do, yet you have this burning desire inside of you that tells you that you want more out of life. That is where I was after I stopped playing basketball and felt lost, with no true direction. I started journaling my thoughts and my emotions every day. When you journal and set time aside to think on your own with no distractions, your mind begins to work in mysterious ways and tends to think of ideas for you to make you grow. I journaled for 30 minutes every day on the rooftop of my dorm and came up with all sorts of crazy ideas!

One of which was to be a real estate developer, which now allows me the freedom to do all the things that I do today. I never knew I wanted to be a real estate developer and never knew anyone who was one. I was journaling on the roof of my college dorm one day and saw a 6-unit apartment building next to my dorm and started to think about all of those units paying the owner of the property rent every month and how much money the owner was probably making off of that building. My goal after basketball was to be rich and to be free. Without journaling every single day, I don't know if I would ever have decided that I wanted to pursue real estate as a career because my mind would not have been focused on wealth and freedom. We underestimate the power of what our brain can come up with when you truly focus on a goal. When you focus and take time to yourself, you will find a way to make whatever you want a reality. For me, it was through real estate.

Your Action Steps

1. Buy a journal.
2. Find a quiet place with ZERO distractions around you.
3. Journal by yourself for at least 30 minutes, four times a week. Build up to journaling seven days a week, but start with four.
4. Write down whatever is on your mind that day! It could be:
   a. New business idea
   b. Argument you went through

      c. Positives and negatives of an idea or a decision you need to make

      d. What you are grateful for

      e. How your day went

      f. Literally anything that comes to your mind

5. Find whatever your biggest public fear is and FORCE yourself to get comfortable with it:

      a. Public speaking

      b. Going out into public

      c. Anything else that inhibits your growth

6. Create a "punishment" for yourself that if you don't do #5 above, you have to do the punishment.

7. Think about #5 EVERY DAY and FORCE yourself out of your comfort zone until it becomes comfortable to you.

Chapter 2 – Doing The Work

When you leave your comfort zone, you will find yourself in situations where you need to learn new things. The only way to do that is to put in the work. There are no shortcuts in life. Yes, you can hire a mentor to learn things quicker and more easily, but at the end of the day you still have to put in the work to learn the things you need to learn. The difference between successful and unsuccessful people is that the successful people are willing to do whatever it takes to make their dreams a reality.

All through my childhood and school years, my dream was to go to the NBA. One quote I heard when I was a kid was, "If I am not working, then somebody else is out there working to take your spot," and I took that to heart. I am a very competitive individual and love to win at everything. So, even when I play a pickup basketball game with my friends, I go hard. I guess I'm just not wired to take it easy, and I do love to win!

In middle school, during my first year of playing basketball, I was terrible! I couldn't dribble a basketball or shoot a jump shot. I did however put in the work every single day to get better and hone my skills so I could excel in the game. I would workout 2-3 times a day since I didn't want there to be a time where I wasn't working and someone else was.

Middle school started at 8 AM, so I would ride my bike to the local YMCA at 5 AM in the morning to get a workout in before I went to school. I would then ride my bike to school, and after school go to basketball practice or ride my bike back to the gym for another workout before heading home. I did that every day. I believed that if I was doing something to better myself every second that I could, then there couldn't be anyone out there working harder than me.

In high school, when I was finally able to drive, I recruited some of my friends and every morning we would drive to Hoover Dam, which has a huge staircase and huge hill that we would run up. We would do all sorts of exercises up and down the staircase and hill until we could barely walk anymore. After a quick stop at home, we would head to the gym and do basketball work outs for the rest of the day. I worked on my game almost every opportunity I got because I wanted to be the best! Through high school, I worked out in the gym and in the weight room every day. I made the varsity high school basketball team when I was just a sophomore.

When I finished high school, I was offered the opportunity to go to Phoenix, Arizona to play basketball for a year at what was basically a Junior College. I left everything I knew back in Columbus, Ohio and flew to Phoenix on my own to pursue my dreams of going to the NBA. When I first got there, I worked out every opportunity I got. I would go to the weight room to lift or would walk down the street to LA Fitness to work out and get some extra shots up whenever I could.

The season started, and I was in the top 1-2 in almost every stat you could be in for our team. But something changed for me and I didn't know what it was. I just started to fall out of love with the game of basketball. It got to a point, towards the end of the season, that I didn't even want to have a basketball in my hand. I stopped working out, stopped going to the gym and basically cut out everything that was basketball and started to be depressed. This happened in the middle of the season, yet I finished the season out as it was something I had already committed to. After that season though, I gave it up entirely. I still had to finish the school year, and without the love of basketball anymore, I found myself in Arizona with no idea what I wanted to do with my life.

Up to that point in my life, all I knew was basketball and I had worked extremely hard at becoming the best basketball player I could be. My dreams were now shattered, and I felt stuck.

So, what did I do?

I went back to what I knew, which was simply putting in the work!

I always loved having money, so the first thing I did was got a valet job in Phoenix. All of my friends were kicking back at the dorms or going out to ASU parties, whereas I would normally be working nights and weekends to save some money. I didn't know what I was saving for, but it all paid off tremendously in the end. I saved as much money as I could and just kept working.

But I was still stuck since I didn't have a passion to pursue in life. So, I started doing things to better myself. As I mentioned in the previous chapter, I bought a journal and started journaling every single day on the roof of my dorm building and I also bought some self-development books to read. Now, I had never been much of a reader, so I don't know what made me want to buy a book and start reading it, but I purchased the book "Think and Grow Rich" by Napoleon Hill from Amazon and had it shipped to the dorm. That book completely changed my life forever! People often ask me where I got my drive in the entrepreneur field from, and a big part of it is due to that book. It opened up my mind to what the possibilities in life could be.

My family wasn't extremely wealthy, but I never had to go without when I was growing up. However, I didn't really see the "rich" side of things, the big houses, the vacations, the nice cars, all the things I thought were reserved for the rich and wealthy. Yet after reading that book and knowing that the riches of the world were for anyone out there to get, I was hooked. I wanted to be extremely successful in the real world.

I journaled and went to work every single day. I picked up all of the overtime shifts I could to save even more money and kept ordering more books looking for that one passion to follow.

I read somewhere that, "90% all of people who file a tax return with a million dollars or more on it had real estate in their portfolio." I don't even know if this is true or not, but it had me hooked. If I had to guess, knowing what I know now, I would say it is accurate. Real estate was going to be my new dream and what I would work on every single day to become the best I could be.

Once I had decided what my passion would be, I started buying real estate books and attending classes. I started reading, googling, and getting on YouTube to watch everything associated with real estate that I could find. I read about owning rental properties, the residual income that comes with it and the equity that you build in your net worth from owning them. I decided that I wanted to buy a rental property, so I continued to save my money.

School finished and it was time for me to pick up everything and move back home to Columbus. I transferred my valet position back to Columbus so I could continue to save as much money as I could. I had promised my mother I would get my college degree, so I started classes at the local community college to deliver on my commitment to her. I also continued to research into real estate and how to purchase a house that made sense as a rental property. I looked at houses on the market every single day in search for the right opportunity.

Finally, I found a duplex on The Ohio State University campus where the cash flow made sense. At the age of nineteen, I put in an offer on a duplex for $243,500 and the offer was accepted. Then reality set in. I did all the research on this project and then it started becoming real and I freaked out. Was I doing this right? Is this really a good deal? Why didn't anyone else purchase this house? I started second guessing myself like crazy, but I decided to follow through and trust my research that I did on real estate and went through and purchased this building.

At this young age, I didn't have a long credit history or a massive amount of income, so I was blessed that my parents decided to co-sign on the loan for me. They had seen all of the work I had done in the past and all of the work I had put in to learn about this new business. It was also a good overall investment, so they decided to help me out.

Yes, I know I was blessed and not everyone has a family member that can co-sign for them. Yet, if my parents had not co-signed on this loan for me, I would have found someone else to co-sign that loan. I would definitely have had to give up equity in the deal to bring someone on board, but people do this all of the time with "equity partners". Equity partners bring in the net worth, the credit, and the income for a deal and get a percentage of the deal in return, and you find the deal, do all of the work, and manage it for your percentage.

Don't let your current situation, family, or upbringing be your excuse for not going out and getting everything you deserve in this world. There is always a way! You just have to get creative and be willing to put in the work.

So, with my parents co-signing the loan, I bought the duplex. It took all of the money that I had saved up till that point. I made this money from cutting grass, shoveling driveways, flipping candy in school, making and selling buckeye necklaces and valeting cars. I put over $30K down on that house and I was broke again. Yet, after all of my expenses every month, I would make about $1,100 in my pocket a month after paying the mortgage on top of my tenants paying down my mortgage every month.

While it was awesome having money that came in without me having to do much work, it was only $1,100 per month. It was going to take me years to save enough money to buy another house similar to this one. I had to find a way to make more money faster so I could replicate this deal. My Realtor on this deal made about $8K on this one house. I said to myself, "Yup, I'm going to go and get my real estate license to save more money so I can buy another house."

I went to real estate school and did the crammer course which took 3 weeks. For three weeks straight, I went to real estate classes from 8 to 5, Monday through Thursday. Most days I also went to school in the evenings as I was taking a full 15-credit hour semester schedule, as well as working my valet job every Friday, Saturday, and Sunday for 10 hours each day. My focus was on saving as much money as I could and educating myself. If you say you don't have enough time to do something, it is simply an excuse in your head that you are telling yourself. Your own thoughts are holding yourself back from pursuing your own dreams. You make time for what you want to make time for!

I got my real estate license and began cold calling clients, trying to find people to buy or sell a house to. I was in the real estate office every day that I wasn't already working or going to school. I was hungry for more. I eventually found two clients looking for houses and I showed them properties they were interested in. After looking at 10-20 houses they decided to buy one. My commission was around $15,000, which was more money than I had seen at one time in my entire life at that point. Yet, I knew deep down that I didn't want to be a Realtor. I wanted to be a real estate investor and developer, so I continued to educate myself in the business.

I went to every real estate meeting I could find in the city. I continued to read books on the subject, educating myself every second I got.

Then, one day I was driving to my valet job and I heard on the radio an ad that said something along the lines of, "If you want to learn how to flip houses, come to our free 2-hour seminar on Saturday. Call this number to sign up."

I whipped out my phone, called the number and reserved my spot at the seminar. I was so excited! The reservation was for two seats, so I told my dad all about it and he decided to come to the seminar with me that weekend!

Every opportunity that came up that required me to learn something new, I didn't hesitate to commit to it and figured the rest of it out on the fly. I was willing to do whatever work was necessary to educate myself and become successful. Between going to school, valeting, starting my real estate business and being a realtor, I was probably working over 100 hours a week.

No matter what the circumstances are, you have to be willing to put in the work and not look for shortcuts. If you put in the work and do what you need to do, things seem to happen to you for the better.

"I don't have enough time," or "I don't have the money," are just lies that people tell themselves. The richest and most successful people in the world have the same twenty-four hours in a day that we do. Time is never an excuse! You can always make time for what you want to make time for, even if that requires you to sleep less. Money is just another excuse. If you stop wasting money on things you don't need or can't afford, then you will have the funds to make an investment when it's needed. Stop taking trips you can't afford. Stop buying clothes you don't need. Start eating ramen noodles and food at home instead of eating out every night. Do that for a few months so you can put away some money in case an opportunity arises that you want to invest in.

Your Action Steps

1. Whatever your passion is, educate yourself in that industry:
   a. Read books on your passion
   b. Go to www.MeetUp.com and search for relevant meetups in your area and GO to *all* of them
   c. Google "Meet ups for (your passion) in (your city)" and GO to *all* of them
   d. Do a YouTube search and watch as many videos as you can on your chosen subject to educate yourself
2. When you go to meetings or seminars, network with people there even if that's hard for you. Get out of your comfort zone. There may be people there who can help you get started or give you opportunities.
3. Decrease your expenses to start saving more money:
   a. Get a roommate (cut expenses in half)
   b. Quit eating out everyday

c. Quit drinking $5 coffees
d. Start a side hustle
e. There are many ways to save money. Go through your expenses and see what you can cut out.

Chapter 3 – Taking The Leap Of Faith

As you work your ass off following your passion, sooner or later an opportunity will present itself to you and it will scare the S*** out of you! The opportunity might look like something you think could end up hurting your finances drastically, you facing the biggest fear of your life, going out on a limb to follow your dreams, or buying into a business opportunity.

Every successful entrepreneur has at some point in their life had to take the leap of faith into the unknown to follow their dreams (some have even done it multiple times). I have been there, had the opportunity of a lifetime with a huge financial investment involved and I had no idea how I was going to come up with the money. Not even taking money into account, I didn't even know what I was going to do after I bought into the opportunity because it was unknown territory.

At the time, it was complete unknown to me and I was nervous, scared of failure, and scared of letting down the people who believed in me. I was doing everything I knew to better myself. I was working every day to save money, educate myself, and grow my income. I was just waiting for my break for that opportunity which would change my life forever.

Hearing that ad for the seminar on the radio was probably one of the best things that has ever happened to me. It was an opportunity like no other. The day of the free seminar, I was working at my valet job, so I met my dad at the hotel where the event was after work. I took a change of clothes with me, dress pants and button up shirt, to make sure I looked my best in case any opportunities came up at this seminar.

Honestly, I thought they were going to choose a few people to work for them and that they would teach those people how to flip houses. That was definitely not the case. There was some good information on how to find undervalued houses and how to flip houses, but the event was really an upsell to their 3-day event, taking place a month later. It was $300 for the three-day event, and when they told us about it, I was the first one to go to the back of the room to sign up to attend. I was so hungry for new information and education. Again, the event was for two people, and my dad agreed to come with me.

For the next month, I didn't really know what to do. I kept working, going to school, learning, and being a Realtor looking for clients – working 100+ hours per week.

The weekend of the conference, I made sure I arrived early and again wore dress pants and a button up shirt to look the part.

Again, I thought they were going to select a few people from the room that they were going to teach how to flip houses. I was wrong again....

There were around 300-400 people in the room and on the first day they gave out lots of great information. I was taking notes like crazy. The second day, more of the same, great information on how to start in this business and how to make money. They were selling a dream of how to make millions in real estate through flipping houses and I was all in. I felt like this was my opportunity to change my life forever.

During day two, they told us about the mentor program that they had. I inched up to the front of my seat and leaned forward as I was so anxious to hear about how I can get involved and really learn the business. They told us about all of the systems, processes, contracts, educational videos, and weekend retreats to teach us the business that they offered if we joined this mentor program.

Then.... Bam! They hit us with it.... The investment was "only" $25,000.

I was devastated. How in the world was I going to come up with $25,000 to join this program? I didn't have the money and had no idea how I was going to make it happen.

But sitting in those seats, I knew this was my opportunity of a lifetime. I had no idea about the real estate business except the one house I kind of threw together and purchased. I had no background in business or construction. I just knew that I was going to figure it out and make it work and that this was my path. I had never felt so strongly about anything in my life than when I was sitting in those chairs.

Was I scared? Absolutely!!! I had no money saved up for this type of immediate investment in myself.

- What if I buy into the mentorship and they don't teach me?
- What if I buy in and I fail?
- What if I pay $25,000 to join the program and never find a house to buy?
- What if I buy in and then can't pay people back?

All of these questions were running through my head and I almost talked myself out of it. But on the flip side, I was also thinking, "What if this does work out?"

- What if I do this and I change the trajectory of my family's life forever?
- What if this really works and my life is never the same again?
- What if this means I can live the life I want to live and help all of the people around me?

I have always heard that the best investment you can make is in yourself...

The positive thoughts started to set in and took a hold of my heart and my mind, and I became even more serious about pursuing this opportunity!

However, there was a catch. The opportunity was only open until the following day. They told us about the mentorship program on day two and on day three you had to come back with all of the money to buy into it. So, in less than 24 hours, I had to come up with $25,000. They offered interview sessions after day two to learn more about the opportunity, so I signed up for one as I still wanted to know exactly what the opportunity was.

I sat down in an interview session and I asked all of the questions:

- How do I know this will work?
- What if I don't find a house?
- What if I fail?
- Do you really do what you say and help people change their life?

At the end of the day, I still believed in my heart that this was the opportunity for me, but I didn't know where to turn or how to make things work. In the interview, they had mentioned that we could pay for the program on a credit card.

Boom! I was in, I was good! I would just open up some credit cards, max them out, and be good to go.

I went home, got online and googled how to apply for credit cards. I found a website where you put in your name, address, how much money you made in a year, and your credit score and they would tell you how much you could be approved for on a credit card.

I was 20-years-old, working as a valet with no previous credit card. I told them I made $100K per year and had a credit score of 800. I may have stretched the truth a little bit... actually, a lot!

They came back and said I was approved for $12,500. I was halfway there!

Now, I had about five thousand dollars in the bank. I was more than halfway there, but I was still short. I went to a few more credit card websites and tried to apply for another credit card, but couldn't get approved for anything else. Again, I was stuck in the water.

So, I turned to everyone I knew and asked them to lend me the other half of the money so I could buy into this program and try to change my life. Some of the feedback I received was:

- "This sounds too good to be true."
- "They might just be selling you a dream."
- "That is a lot of money, Austin."
- "I don't know about this."
- "Maybe next time they are in town."
- "Save some more money for the next opportunity."

On one side, I am all in, ready to make it happen, and on the other, I'm crushed because I couldn't find the money and the opportunity was going down the drain. Talk about an emotional roller coaster! Having the people around you that you care about and trust not be 100% in sucked, but I understood. This was just simply a dream that I was chasing, and it was a huge investment into something that was completely unknown.

I love my family to death, and they have always believed in me and supported me in everything that I have done in my life. They bought me basketballs and shoes when I needed them, traveled to tournaments with me, and sent me to school in Phoenix for a year, which I know wasn't cheap. I didn't feel slighted, but it was disappointing that this opportunity was falling through the cracks. What I came to realize though is that it's not that they didn't believe in me, because I know they did, they simply didn't know any better. For most, when something like this is offered, "give me

$25K and I will teach you how to make millions", it is normally a scam and too good to be true.

All night I tried to figure out how to come up with the remaining money so I could buy into the program the next day.

One in the morning came around and I remember how I felt, and I was about to give up...I felt crushed, lost, and alone. I didn't know what else to do to make this happen by tomorrow. I was still living with my parents at the time. I literally crawled under my parents dining room table and chairs and began to cry because I truly felt I was missing out on my opportunity of a lifetime. I didn't know when something like this might come around again. Later, it came out that it wasn't a little sniffle cry, it was one of those real cries where everyone can hear it.

But I am blessed to this day for my parents and can't ever thank them enough!!!! They came downstairs and offered to put in the other half of the investment for me so I could move forward and invest in the program the next day and chase my dreams.

I don't know if I slept for the rest of the night as I had crazy mixed emotions. I was happy, excited, and also nervous and scared of the unknown all at the same time. I really didn't know if I was going to be successful and whether I would be able to pay my parents back what they had invested into me. I started questioning myself again and asking myself if this was really such a good idea?

The last day of the conference came and anyone paying for the program was asked to go to the back of the room. My parents and I slowly walked to the back of the room; we asked some more questions to make sure we were all still on board.

The next thing you know, I was in! I swiped my credit card and maxed it out, my parents swiped their credit card for the other half of the investment and now I was really scared. I had made the jump into the unknown without a true plan on how to make it in the business. It felt like I jumped into a black hole, but I knew that with the education that was now available to me and the coaching calls, manuals, and educational videos, it would get me there! It was more debt than I had ever had to my name in my whole life. There were eighteen months of no interest on my credit card, so I knew I had that much time to pay everything back before the payments went crazy and I would have to start paying 15-20% interest on the debt, which I would really not be able to afford. I also knew I had to make it in this business so I could pay my parents back and not make them regret lending me the money, which motivated me even more.

Some years later, I asked my parents why they decided to lend me that money after they told me no at first.

What they told me was, "We have watched you grow up and pursue every opportunity you had with everything that was in you. When you would shovel driveways and cut the neighborhoods grass to make money when your friends were out having fun, when you created an entire supply chain in middle school in our garage on making buckeye necklaces, riding your bike to the park to pick up buckeyes, washing them, drilling holes in them, buying beads and necklace rope, and stringing them all together, paying your friends for every necklace that they made, and going to the OSU football games to sell them. In basketball, you worked harder than anyone we had ever known. We got to thinking about why we would respect you and support you for all of that hard work and tell you no on something like this. Then when we heard you crying, we knew you were all in and would do whatever it took to make it work."

I cannot thank them enough for the opportunities they have provided me, but don't let that be an excuse for you if you are thinking, "I don't have anyone that would do that for me." I know people who joined that same mentor program, who are now friends of mine, that decided to partner up with 3 different people to buy into the program together, so it was only $6,250 per person. One of my best friends started their real estate business from watching YouTube videos and is crushing it right now! There is ALWAYS a way to make something happen if you really put in the time and energy to find a way to make it happen. Don't let a situation or your upbringing be your excuse for not chasing your dreams!

Work your ass off every day of your life so when an opportunity does arise, you will have people around you that have seen how hard you work and will believe and invest in you!

Once I was in the program, I had to start working and educating myself all over again! I dove right into the education material and went to all of the conferences to learn everything I could. But, by one month, two months, three months, six months, nine months later, still no results. I had not purchased a house or raised any money, and most importantly, I had not made a penny in the business! It would eventually pay off tenfold, but it took over a year to make a single penny in the business! (In the next chapter, I'll detail all of my success and the ending to this story)

I could tell you numerous stories of people who were scared to death of the unknown and going all in on pursuing their dreams, who then finally took that jump and absolutely love their life now and are so happy that they did!

If you want some motivation to take that leap of faith in your own life, sign up to my email list at www.FlippingTheRightWay.com. This will provide you with information about growing your business, real estate, and most importantly, changing your mindset. There is also advice on running a business, and the real struggles and accomplishments that I go through every day to keep you motivated!

At some point in your life, an opportunity will be presented to you. It may be a mentorship, it may be a job opportunity, or it may be giving up everything you grew up around and flying across the country. You need to be ready and willing to take that leap of faith and follow your dreams. It will be scary, and you might not know what to do or where to turn. But you will feel that this is the opportunity that you need to take and need to commit to. Know in your heart that you will figure everything else out, but make sure you don't miss your opportunity and regret it for the rest of your life!

Your Action Steps

1. Believe that opportunity will come and that you will be ready to make the jump!
2. Make sure that you are preparing yourself and working for the opportunity. The opportunity won't just show up. You

will need to educate yourself in your passion, go to networking opportunities, and introduce yourself to people in the industry as they may just be the ones with the opportunity for you.

Chapter 4 – The Grind And Disappointment

You make the jump into the unknown to follow your dreams and sometimes things don't work out exactly how you thought they were going to. That's life! Things rarely ever go according to your plan. If it was easy, everyone would do it. You are going to hit roadblock after roadblock through your whole life.

You are going to have to change your mindset to get through all of those roadblocks. You are going to be so excited to be chasing your dreams and then you will get smacked in the face, I promise you. The difference between successful and unsuccessful people is that the successful people have gotten up more times and tried again more times than the unsuccessful people have. Some people fall down and never get back up. One little set back and they're done. You have to get it into your head that you are going to grind it out as long as it takes until you make your dreams a reality.

I remember very vividly the months that followed me buying into that mentor program. I thought I was going to find a great deal in the first couple months and make all of my money back, and I would make a few hundred thousand dollars within the first twelve months and life would be great. After three months passed and I didn't have any traction or any solid leads on houses that I could renovate and sell for a profit, I started to feel discouraged. I felt that maybe I had made a bad decision and now I had set myself and my family up with a ton of debt that I couldn't pay off.

Yet, I continued reading and I learned about the power of manifestation. Manifestation is basically thinking things into existence. You can envision things in your mind and the more you think about it and believe it, the more ways your brain looks for solutions to that problem and eventually it turns into reality.

What I did was I created "The most perfect day I could imagine" in my mind. Every single day I would envision what my perfect day would be. I would sit in a quiet place by myself and envision myself going through my perfect day. As you try this, truly think about it and get emotionally attached to what your day looks like. The more emotions you tie to it, the more it will begin to become real and the more your brain will begin to come up with ways of creating that perfect day.

Every day that I struggled and was not getting to where I wanted to be, I envisioned my perfect day. Me, living in the brand-new house that I built, waking up and walking into a massive master bathroom to get ready, going downstairs to the gym inside my house and getting a morning workout in. I would then make breakfast in my open concept kitchen with a huge island that opens up into the living room where I could watch TV. After breakfast, I would go back upstairs and shower in a huge shower with body jets and multiple shower heads, getting ready in my huge walk in closet. I would journal on the balcony off the master bedroom, read a book looking out over my 3-car garage, pool, hot tub, and basketball court in the backyard. When it was time to leave the house, I'd walk into my 3-car garage and have a choice of cars to drive to work, an all blacked out Range Rover or Rolls Royce. I would be free to choose whether I would go into the office for a few hours or just do whatever I wanted to do during the day or go on vacation whenever I wanted to.

I envisioned this every night when I went to bed and this kept me driven to continue to go after my dreams and not give up on everything when things weren't working out.

I can remember wanting to quit many times during my journey. It took me over 16 months from the day I bought into the program to make a single penny in the real estate business. I was broke that entire time working my ass of every day.

The day after buying into the program, I got online and started listening to their courses on how to flip houses so I could learn as quickly as possible. It was a wealth of information and I didn't know where to start at the beginning, so the first thing I did is what they suggested: I started marketing to sellers for properties that I could buy.

At this time, I was putting all of my spare time into learning this new business as well as continuing to put in around 60 hours per week at my valet job, going to college in the evenings to get my degree, and showing people houses as a realtor. Except for a short time every day to sleep, I was working every second of every day.

I was continuously researching and looking at houses whenever I could. I sat in the basement of my parents' house for hours, writing hand addressed letters to sellers to try to get them to sell me their house. There would be hundreds if not thousands of letters to address, fold and stamp every single week.

After a short sleep, I would wake up and head downtown at seven in the morning for work. I did this every day! There was one time when I was driving home on a Sunday afternoon, completely exhausted and I fell asleep at the wheel. As my car hit the curb and went up onto the sidewalk, I woke up and saw a light pole directly in front of me. It was about ten feet away from me. I immediately swerved the car back onto the road and thankfully missed the light pole. When I got home, I went right back to writing the letters that needed to be ready to be sent out Monday morning.

I didn't start to feel bad for myself or take a nap or give up on my dreams. I had a bigger vision for my life than living paycheck to paycheck, and that was the dream that I was chasing – freedom. If I had quit, I would have been doing a huge disservice to the people that had believed in me. When you quit on your dreams, you're not just giving up on yourself, but you are quitting on everyone who has ever helped you progress in your life. You are quitting on your family, your friends, everyone. Without your success, you won't be able to change your life or the lives of the people around you.

For ten months straight, I worked, went to school, tried to start my real estate business every day looking at houses. I did not buy a single house during that time. Finally, I caught a break and a seller returned one of my phone calls and said he was interested in selling his house. His property was in an extremely hot part of town and he was asking a very reasonable price, so I set up an appointment immediately.

On the day of the appointment, I went to the house to meet the seller. We talked about him, his family, the house, and what he needed out of it. We agreed on a purchase price for the house and signed an agreement.

When I got home, I was more excited than ever. However, I was also extremely nervous. Doubt started to creep back into my mind right after another exciting opportunity. I started to question myself.

- Was I overpaying for the house?
- Would I be able to raise the money I would need to buy and renovate this house?
- Could I really do all of this at 21-years-old?
- What if I lost money?
- Why hadn't anyone else purchased this house?

Even with all of that doubt and fear, I didn't allow it to stop me and I pressed on. I picked up the phone and called a friend that I had met whilst networking at one of the real estate meetings I went to. I asked if he would walk through this house with me, confirm that I was not crazy and that this was a good investment and would be profitable. He confirmed everything.

Now I had to find a way to raise $230,000 in private money in three weeks. At the time I was 21 years old and had to figure out how I could convince someone to give me their entire retirement fund and trust me to buy, renovate, and sell this house for a profit when I didn't have any previous experience in the business.

I started calling the list of potential private lenders that I had put together. In one day of calling people nonstop, I had raised all of the money to fund the purchase and rehab of the house.

I purchased that house for $74,000 and put roughly $170,000 into the rehab. I don't know about everywhere else, but in Columbus, Ohio, you could build an entire new house with that sort of budget and this was just for the renovation of a house. We renovated every imaginable part of that house. We tore it down to the studs, reframed the entire house, built a new foundation and a 600-square foot addition on the house. We also built a 2-car garage, replaced the entire sewer line, and gave the house a brand-new exterior as well.

I had no background in construction... yet, I trusted the process. Did I plan for all of the renovation work? Absolutely not! There were many surprises that I didn't plan for, but I figured it out. I put some more of my own money into the deal and I called one of my lenders and asked for more money to get the job done. My contractor disappeared at the end of the job and it was like pulling teeth to get him back to the job to get the job completed. All of these things I didn't plan for and didn't know how to handle, but I figured everything out.

Finally, it was the last week of the job. I was trying to tie up all the loose ends, but I couldn't get my contractor back to the job. He said he was done! I ended up working on the house myself until the early hours of the morning, and then sleeping on the couch that was in the house. I did this for several days to get the house finished so that we could list it for sale.

The house was done!

By now, it had been fifteen months of working in this business, not making a single penny and setback after setback. There were times where I had less than $200 in my bank account and I was hundreds of thousands of dollars in debt with monthly payments going out every month. I had put every dollar I had into this new business and this house. It seemed like one thing after another kept going wrong and I had to keep putting more and more money into the project.

I finally listed the house for sale and had 8 offers on the house in less than 10 hours of it being on the market. Finally, something was going right!

I sold the house thirty days later and after paying off all of my lenders, contractors, debt, insurance, and expenses, I walked away with $103K in my pocket. At the age of twenty-one, I had made my first 6-figures and felt like I was on top of the world.

Yet the vision in my head was bigger than just making one hundred thousand dollars. That wasn't even remotely close to what my goals were. I had seen my perfect day in my head every single day for sixteen months and knew that this was just the beginning.

I paid off all the debt that I owed (except for the mortgage on my rental property) and reinvested ALL of the remaining profit back into my business. I did not buy a single thing for myself. I continued to work over 60 hours a week valeting, going to college and grinding away in my real estate business. Many people would have celebrated with a new watch or a new car, but when you have a dream so ingrained into your brain, you don't allow any distractions into your life and you go ALL IN on your business to achieve it!

It took me about six weeks to find and purchase my next property. It took me four months to buy, renovate, and sell that house for a profit and I personally made another $40K on that deal after paying everyone. I also had another house under contract that I was going to purchase within the next 30 days.

For twenty months straight, I visualized my dream life in my head every single night. I believed in it so much in my heart that there wasn't anything that could deter me from obtaining and reaching my goals. There are always going to be lots of ups and downs along the path of the entrepreneurial journey. You can't give into those downs; that is what everyone expects you to do. The majority of people in this world give up on their dreams before they even try to take action towards them. Of the very small number of people that take that initial jump into the unknown to follow their dreams, I would guess that more than half of those quit within the first 3 months because they don't make the money they were expecting, and they get pushed down by business and life. If being an entrepreneur was easy, everyone would do it

Life eventually comes full circle. I had visualized my perfect day every day for almost five years. At the time of writing this book, I had completed building my new house and moved in a couple months ago. It had everything that I wanted my "perfect" day to have: gym, balcony, kitchen, master bathroom, home office, etc. There is no pool in the back yard, but it does have a hot tub.

The only reason I didn't put a pool in was that the plot of land wasn't big enough as I wanted to live downtown, and space was limited. Just after I moved in, I also purchased a new all blacked out Range Rover that is parked in my three-car garage along with my motorcycle and Jaguar. Everything that I envisioned came true. The only thing that is missing is a pool in my back yard and a Rolls Royce in my garage. I am however in negotiations for a bigger piece of land downtown on which I will build my new dream house and the Rolls Royce is coming soon as well... follow me on IG @AustinRutherfordOfficial to see the journey.

When you visualize your perfect day, you have to truly believe in your heart that you can achieve that lifestyle. You can't just briefly go over it and say it in your mind. You have to envision that lifestyle and your "perfect" day every single day and believe that in your heart it will be yours. Be so stuck on achieving that goal that no set back along your journey can stop you. Your belief and willpower will get you through the ups and downs of the business and will keep you focused on that bigger goal. No obstacles will get in your way with this mind set.

Remember, however, that when you achieve your "perfect" day, you need to update your goal in your head to achieve something even bigger!

Your Actions Steps

1. Write out your "perfect" day in your journal:

a. Write out vivid and detailed sentences that describe exactly what you want and who you are with when living that day.

b. Every morning and evening visualize yourself living your perfect day. Make sure you have a quiet space to focus on this.

c. Commit to not being deterred from your goals until you achieve that "perfect" day. It will keep you motivated through the low times and disappointments.

Chapter 5 – Stay In Your Own Lane

One of the questions I get asked all of the time is, "Knowing what you know now, what would you have done differently at the beginning?"

Everyone has their own journey that they have to go through in order to get to where they want to be. Everyone's upbringing and situations are always different, and you can't compare your journey to someone else's.

Before I get to some of the things that I would have done differently, I want to stress that you can't compare where you are in your life to where anyone else is. They could have been born into a multi-million-dollar business or could have worked hard for twenty years to get where they are today. Don't compare a 20-year-old just starting a business to someone who has been in the business for more than 25 years with many employees.

Comparisons will drive you crazy. You will never make yourself happy doing it, as there will always be someone with more money, more freedom, more of everything that you want.

You have to figure out what *you* want in your life!

Some people want hundreds of millions of dollars, and there are major sacrifices needed to grow a business that big, including massive time commitments which will likely strain your relationships with your loved ones. Other people want to make $5-10million per year, which after a lot of hard work in the first few years, will allow you to achieve that level so you have time and freedom for yourself and your loved ones. Finally, there are people who just want a 9-5 job making $40,000-$80,000 per year without the stress of being an entrepreneur, making the tough decisions and running the risk of not being able to pay the bills

There is no right or wrong answer here!

You have to decide what you want in your life. Nobody else can decide that for you. Take some time and journal on exactly what you want your life to look like. Build your goals around your answer!

So, what would I have done differently if I had known what I know now?

First, I would not have been comparing myself to other businesses out there, especially when they had been in business for many years. I am a competitive person and never like to lose. Sometimes I was too focused on my competition, rather than focusing on my own business and building the life that I wanted.

Secondly, I would have hired people into my business a lot earlier than I actually did. You can only do so much in a day. Once your business gets started and you have some money to pay people, you need to hire people to do the non-income producing tasks. Continue to do the high-income producing tasks until you can afford to pay people to do those as well. Non-incoming producing tasks are still incredibly important aspects of your business, but you should be spending your time on negotiating contracts, negotiating sales, prospecting for new clients, etc. rather than sitting behind your desk tracking a spreadsheet for a marketing campaign. Prioritize tasks which produce income for the business.

I had trouble "letting go" of my business at first. My mentor for almost a year and a half told me I needed to hire an assistant to take some of the duties off of my plate, but I couldn't "let go" of my business. I would work all day in the field and then all afternoon, evening, and into the next morning sometimes on the office work on the things that 100% needed to get done, the marketing, accounting, scrapping lists, paperwork, etc. These things could have been hired out long before I ever got around to it. Eventually, I gave in and hired an assistant to help with the many tasks that were on my plate and she kills it. One of the best decisions I ever made!

I then had more time to negotiate more contracts, talk with more sellers, and buy more deals which eventually led to making more money.

Thirdly, I would have aimed higher from the beginning. My goal was to make $100,000 a year and, looking back now, that goal was WAY too small. My growth at the beginning was really slow because my goals were too small. Knowing what I know now, I would have set my sights much higher. Consider the difference: you aim for $100,000 and come up short by only making $70,000 vs shooting to make $1,000,000 and coming up short and making $700,000. In both examples, you made 70% of your goal. However, with the second goal you made a lot more money. You can't achieve anything if your mind doesn't already believe it. Push yourself and shoot for that outlandish goal and take the risks you maybe wouldn't take if your goals were much smaller. You will grow much faster!

Your Actions Steps

1. Stop comparing yourself to others.
2. Decide what you want. Write down what you want your life to be like and what will make you happy and design your business around that lifestyle.
3. Always go bigger then you think you can achieve at that moment.
4. Hire out tasks that produce no income as soon as you can:
   a. If you are already in a business, making some money:
      i. Make an Excel spreadsheet with 15-minute intervals throughout the day
      ii. For a week, track everything you do every day in 15-minute intervals
      iii. After seven days, review the results and put a dollar amount against each task that you

would be willing to pay someone else to do that task.

    iv. Hire someone to cover those tasks to free up your time.

b. If you haven't started your business yet, you will have to do everything in the beginning, but once you start making some money, do the exercise above.

Chapter 6 – Change Your Mindset On Money

You may be making a little money or maybe you are dead broke, yet you want more out of life. As you grew up, you were taught that going to college was normal, that working a 9-5 job your whole life was a necessity to survive, or maybe even that having a lot of money was not a good thing.

You are going to have to change your mindset on money. Having money and having an abundance of it is not a bad thing! I don't agree that money is the root of all evil. I do believe that the LOVE of money, the continuous chase for more and the willingness to do anything for money, is the root of all evil. You are doing a disservice to your family and the people around you to not go out into this world and make as much money as legally possible.

Without money, you can't take your family on vacations and show them the world. You will not be able to give back to people in your life that have helped you along your path, your parents, family, mentors etc. Finally, and maybe the most selfish, if you do not go out and create wealth, you are not able to give back to the people in need or to change someone else's life forever!

I love money! I also love having money, but I still know the difference between right and wrong.

Whether you are just starting your journey or have a little bit of money, feeling guilt towards having money or chasing after it is a very real thing. I know I used to believe that "rich" people either inherited it or had screwed over a lot of people to get it, and that they were bad people. Now I know that simply is not the case.

A little over a year ago, I wanted to buy a new car. I had been driving an old Toyota Camry around for years. I had never really bought myself anything nice up to this point. Deep down I knew why. I felt guilty about having money when most of the people around me didn't have any. Nobody really had a real abundance of money when I was growing up.

I used to think, "What if I buy a new car and my friends start to look at me differently and despise me for having a nice car?" Or "Would my family be envious of me for having something nicer than they had?", or even that everyone in this world would look at a young 21-year-old and talk down to me, saying I was selfish, arrogant, or cocky because I had some nice things.

I thought about this often, so for years, I never bought anything nice for myself because of that guilt I felt inside.

One day I found enough courage and went up to a car dealership to look at cars. They didn't have what I wanted on the lot, so I told them I wanted an Audi A7 or a Jaguar XJL, and the price range I wanted to pay. They said they would call me once they got anything in.

About a month later, I got a call from the dealer saying that they had just got one of the cars on the lot. It was actually towards the lower end of my budget, but they had someone else going to look at it the next day. I was super excited as this is exactly what I wanted, so I jumped in the car and started heading to the dealership.

For the entire first half of that drive I was doubting myself, asking myself if I really needed this car or whether it was a good idea. Doubt and guilt crept into my mind and I almost talked myself out of it. I picked up the phone and called my mentor, Mark Evans, and explained to him how I felt and what was going through my head. What he told me changed my life forever...

He said, "Austin, the world and society wants to make you feel guilty for having nice things because they aren't willing to put the work in to obtaining those things. Instead, they want to talk you out of chasing those things in hopes you won't either. It is always easier for someone to say it's not possible or to talk down to someone who is willing or has put in the work because that is the easy way out for them. By saying this, they feel that they don't have to put in all of the hard work to change their life, as they can continue to play small and just make others feel guilty for doing those things. Putting in the work, not feeling defeated and quitting, and attaining your goals is hard! That is why only a few people are actually able to live the life they want."

Then I asked him, "What if I buy it and people around me stop doing business with me, start charging me more, or feel differently towards me?"

He responded with, "If people around you start feeling that way then they shouldn't be around you because you never want people around you that are hoping for you to fail and people who talk down to you are never going to add any value to your life, so their opinions are irrelevant to you. You have worked your ass off for this goal, you deserve it so go and buy the damn car."

I finished the drive to the dealership and drove off the lot with a new car that day and have never looked back! Since then, I have bought some nice things and I have realized that there are two types of people in this world. Those that hate on people with nice things and I don't ever take their opinions into consideration. The other group are those that are motivated by other people that have nice things and that is what I do it for now, to motivate others! For me, I love seeing people winning because I use that as a driving factor and makes me see what else is possible out there. If another living breathing human being can do it, why can't I? I only surround myself with those people that see nice things and are motivated by those things to achieve.

It still blows my mind that to this day, anytime a conversation about money is brought up, that everyone always shy's away from it. It is like we are taught to not talk about money and it is evil or something.

I love to talk about money. I even loved to talk about money when I was broke! I didn't have any but I talked about it all of the time. Again, the things that are in your life and that you surround yourself with tend to become real and enter your life.

People sometimes ask me, "Why do you talk about money so much?"

My answer is always for two reasons.

One is I believe that if you never talk about money in your life, you will never have any. I believe so strongly that money is a good thing and can be used for an incredible purpose for myself and the people around me that I talk about it often because I know the more I surround myself with it and the more I believe in it, the more money that will come to me!

The second reason is to motivate and inspire myself and the ones around me. When I was broke, some people saw my vision board of all of the things that I wanted and it got them to think deeper about what they could achieve in this life and got some people to change their goals and their mindsets to achieve more. I would talk with my mentors every chance I could about money and how they made it which inspired me to go even harder! Now, when I talk about money or a big deal that I'm closing, I get DMs on Instagram or private messages on Facebook saying, "Keep inspiring us," or "I love watching your stories because it motivates me every single day to get better," or a message I got today, "I keep telling you this but you truly keep motivating me to be out of my comfort zone and I know the payoffs will be coming soon. Please under no circumstances stop posting things like this."

Money is not a negative thing it can be phenomenal if used correctly. Use the conversation around money to motivate yourself and to motivate the people around you as well and it will start to flow in like you couldn't even imagine. You have a duty to go out into the world and earn as much money as you can, so you can live the life that you are destined to live and give back to the people that helped you.

Your Action Steps

1. Don't let people make you believe that having money is a negative thing.
    a. When people talk down about people with money, it is simply their limiting beliefs. It is what they think life should be and they are simply trying to hold you back. Don't let their limiting beliefs become real in your life.
2. When you've earned money in your business, buy yourself nice things. You deserve it!

Chapter 7 – Be Careful Who You Surround Yourself With

As you pursue your dream, I have to tell you that you are going to lose some of the closest people in your life. Some of your friends, and even some family members, won't agree with what you are doing. They may think that obtaining your goal is simply not possible and may try to talk you out of it or talk negatively about it in the hope that you will give up on your dream.

Remember, the power of thinking things into existence? The more negative energy you have surrounding you, the more negative things will come into your life. If you surround yourself with positive people who are looking to better themselves and who talk positively about everything then positive things will come into your life. Be very careful about the people you allow into your life and who you spend time with.

Not everyone is meant to be in your life! You have to surround yourself with people that are going to help you obtain your goal or motivate you and be in your corner to encourage you to keep chasing your dreams. Chasing your dreams is hard and if you allow negativity around you, then when things start going bad, those negative people start saying, "I told you so," or "Why can't you just trust me that this isn't possible," and you may believe them and give up on everything. However, if you have people that keep encouraging you, who understand what you are going through and continue to tell you it is possible and it is all worth it, then it is more likely you will keep going after your dreams.

Look at all your family and friends and ask yourself, "Do these people support me or do they hold me back?" I am not saying that you need to cut people off completely, but for those people who don't support you or who are always being negative, you need to have a conversation with them. Tell them you need support and positive vibes from them or limit the time you spend around them. Start spending time with like-minded people who want to better their lives and with mentors who are already in the position that you want to be in.

Look to spend time with positive people that are following their dreams. There will be so much positivity around you that you will always stay motivated. Find people when you are at events that want success and freedom just like you. Even if these people are not passionate in the same field as you, having people around you that encourage you, who see more in you then you see in yourself, who hold you accountable and don't let you quit on yourself is priceless!

Finding a mentor is not always easy. People who could mentor you, that are in the position that you want to be in, are normally extremely busy and may be very particular about who they spend their time with. Here are a couple of stories about how I met my mentors, however, remember not everyone you approach will become your mentor.

When I was still in high school chasing my basketball dreams, I was working out one Saturday morning in the gym getting in an extra workout. During the workout, Mr. Amerson, the weight room coach, asked if anyone was interested in working nights, driving around the city to pass out flyers at $10 per hour. Some people in the weight room looked at him like he was crazy, but I jumped up immediately and said I was in and asked when I started.

I was used to putting in extra work so working a few extra hours on Thursday, Friday, and Saturday night was perfectly fine with me. I didn't even think about missing out on the weekends or not spending time with friends. I was hungry and wanted that extra money!

Mr. Amerson introduced me to Mike Matalka, who to this day is one of my mentors and very good friends. Later that week, I drove out to Mike's office and picked up a huge box of flyers. When I got there, he was really busy on the phone and talking to his employees. He asked me how I knew Mr. Amerson and then gave me the box of flyers. He told me when and where the flyers needed to be handed out and I was on my way. I worked for him for several months. I never missed a day passing out those flyers, was always on time, and every time I came back into the office, he had a little more time for me and we got to know each other better. I was intrigued and loved business and always wanted to know more about how successful people made it, so I asked him about his company and how he worked himself up to the position he had.

Then one week, he said he no longer needed those flyers passed out. My first thought was that I was losing my income stream, but more importantly, I wasn't going to have the chance to ask him any questions anymore. We talked briefly as I was leaving. Then, I just straight up asked him, "If I have a business idea or need to talk about anything, you mind if I give you a call?" Luckily, he said yes, and we continue to talk at least once a month to this day.

If I had to ask him why he gave up his time for me, I would guess his answer would be that Mr. Amerson spoke very highly about my work ethic, that I was respectful and always on time, that I always did what was required, and that I asked the right questions about his business. But out of all those reasons, the most important would be the simple fact that he wanted to help. Most successful people want to give back and help others. Granted, they normally just don't have the time, so if you can add value to them and get them emotionally attached, they will normally make time for you.

With any mentor, you will have to add an immense amount of value to their life before they may feel inclined to help you back. Give your time to them for free and help them in any way, shape, or form even if you just have to run errands for them. I remember driving down to Buckeye Lake, which was about an hour away, to pick up a car for him and driving it back to Columbus for his dealership. I remember going to his pizza shop for him, and even going to the car auction with him because he needed an extra driver to drive one of the cars back. I did all of this for free. I wanted to add as much value to his life as I could because I knew that nine times out of ten, it comes back full circle! It did, and he is now a really good friend who I can call on for anything!

When meeting with possible mentors, a great question to ask is, "What can I do to make your life easier? How can I add value to you?" If they need something done, and you openly put yourself out there like that, then they may ask you to do something for them. Keep in mind, they may say "nothing" at first, but if you continue to follow up, adding value to them in any way that you can, eventually they will give in and ask you for something and then you are in!

The second person I want to tell you about is my mentor Mark Evans. I met him at a real estate meetup years ago and I was doing business with some mutual friends at the time. He was coming to Columbus to speak at the meet up for a few hours. The title company I was working with to close our deals, also closed his deals as well. They suggested that I meet this guy as he was doing an insane amount of business compared to what I was doing at the time. Always hungry to learn, I went along.

I listened to everything he had to say and then introduced myself to him at the end of the event. I thanked him for his speech and the inspiration I received from listening to him. He started telling me about all of the nice things the title company had said about me. How I was hungry for growth, hardworking, kind, etc.

It's always nice to hear other people speaking highly about you, but always remember that how you treat people and your work ethic will always come full circle. If you treat people badly then, that will get around. On the flipside, if you are hungry and willing to learn, that will get around as well. The other lesson here is to not be scared about introducing yourself to people. Sometimes we put people on a pedestal just because they have more money than us or that they are more successful than us, but they are human, too! Don't be nervous. Talk to them, introduce yourself and ask them one or two solid questions that you want to know answers to. They will respect you for that!

A couple of days later, Mark called me and asked if I wanted to come to a Mastermind a few weeks later in Cleveland with ten other very high-level real estate investors and I immediately said that I was in. Since then, we have become very good friends, have traveled together, and talk a few times every month.

Anytime I hear anything about real estate, I always introduce myself as you never know what opportunities you may uncover. Don't be shy, put yourself out there and get to know people.

Malon, one of my best friends today, and I have a very similar story on how we met and how we added value to one another's life. I was in the basketball gym to play some pickup games and walked by a bench where I heard someone say to his friend, "Yeah, I just wholesaled a house last week." Wholesaling is a real estate investor term of making money, so I immediately stopped and introduced myself to him and told him what I did.

I had heard his name in the past from other investors, and he had also heard good things about me around town. He was my age and the conversation was great. He said we should grab lunch sometime on him. I often get asked to meet up with people so that they can pick my brain and learn about the business. Normally, I don't do these meetings because they usually aren't serious and I don't always have the time as I am still growing my business and myself. I enjoyed our short conversation at the gym. I was always looking to surround myself with like-minded people and knew we both had value to add one another, so I was in.

Since that lunch meeting, he is now one of my best friends, we talk almost daily, travel together multiple times per year and hang out almost every weekend. I have added a ton of value to his life in the real estate space and he has added immense value to my life, helping me shape my mindset and how I carry myself. To this day, he is one of the most positive people in my life. He has built up the confidence in my head tenfold and I am forever grateful to him for that.

Malon is a perfect example of keeping people around you that are really positive and who believe in you more than you believe in yourself! I know for a fact I wouldn't have the confidence I walk in today or some of the business opportunities I have today if I hadn't have had him in my life encouraging me and putting positive vibes into my life every single time I talk with him.

Seeking and finding a mentor is all based on the value that each party gives to each other. I have gone to lunch many times with people to let them "pick my brain" and never speak to them ever again. Lunch with Malon was completely different as there was a massive exchange of value. He changed how I thought about things, which is why even today I can pick up the phone at any time and know he is there for me. The other two mentors are also now my friends, who I can call at any time. I have given value to their lives at every opportunity I can because I know how important it is to bring value to any relationship.

Add value to others in any way you can and always set a good example of yourself no matter where you are. Those examples, negative or positive, always have a way of coming full circle and helping you or hurting you. Always seek first to give and add value to others, especially people you are hoping will become your mentors, before EVER asking for anything in return. Give, give, give, and give some more so that when you do ask for 10, 30, 60 minutes of their time to ask the questions you want to ask, then they feel inclined to help you in return.

When looking for a mentor, do your research on them, find out what is important to them, and where possible, build that information into your giving value to them. Maybe they have a favorite restaurant? Suggest it as the venue for lunch. Be creative and think outside the box so that people will remember you.

One other quick life hack when trying to seek out a mentor: If they love a certain type of liquor, or have a favorite sports team, send them something unique that will catch their attention like their bottle of liquor or a poster to their favorite sports team, thanking them for taking their time (even if it was one minute at a meet up) for talking with you. Send them a decanter with their logo on it, or tickets to a local sports team that they like.

Be creative and think outside the box. All of those things mentioned above add value and I promise you they probably mean more to these people then you think. Doing something out of the box like that means you put time into thinking about it. They will know that when they receive the gift, they will most likely feel inclined to give you some of their time in return when you go over and beyond.

When you do get that 30-60-minute meeting, make sure to limit your time with them to the agreed upon 30-60 minutes and they will respect you and most likely give you the time of day in the future.

Another great tip is to ALWAYS send a handwritten letter to a new mentor you are seeking to foster a relationship with, thanking them for the time. People very rarely receive handwritten letters anymore. You will stand out from the crowd and they will remember you took the time to write them a personal letter!

Your Action Steps

1. Go to meet ups and seek to introduce yourself to people who are already in the position you want to be in.
2. Use the questions, "What can I do to make your life easier? How can I add value to you?" to establish how to add value to their life.
3. Always give before asking for anything in return.
4. Remember to say thank you in a personal manner, and be creative about it.

Chapter 8 – The Power Of Affirmations

As I mentioned in the previous chapter, going to lunch with Malon changed my life dramatically in many different ways. Most importantly, he saw something in me that I had doubted in myself for my entire life.

Since I was a kid, I have always doubted myself. While I had confidence and knew that I would make it and was making some money, I struggled to hit my full potential because there was always something in me that doubted myself. What Malon taught me was to have unwavering confidence in myself and no matter where I was to know I bring value in any room.

I can remember standing in a room and not introducing myself to other people because I thought that they had more money than me so I couldn't offer them any value. No matter what space you are in, there is always some value you can offer. No one has been through the same experiences as you and not everyone has the same outlook on life's situations.

Back in high school, I would attend school dances and I would never actually dance. I would just stand against the wall and watch the rest of the room having fun because I didn't know how to dance. I was worried about what other people would say if I started dancing and it didn't look right. Scared of people judging me or making fun of me, I wouldn't go out on the dance floor at all because of fears that I created in my head that probably didn't even exist.

It's difficult to act like that if you surround yourself with the right people. Every day I would talk to Malon and he would pump me up. He would tell me how I was the man, killing the game, had so much more to achieve and how much more I had in the tank. He made me realize what everyone has in themselves. You can be anything *you* want to be and do anything you want to do; you just have to visualize it for yourself.

I started saying positive affirmations to myself every day. I also created a vision board of my goals so that I could see it multiple times every day.

An affirmation is something you tell yourself that may or may not be true... yet... but that you want to be true in the future. Here are some of my affirmations I say to myself every morning:

1. I am extremely confident in myself and my values, I don't need anybody else's approval!
2. I am running my multi-million-dollar business from all over the world. My team is on the ground and I have full trust in

them and am confident they have the skills and tools to be successful!

3. I command the room when I walk in. I carry my shoulders high and I am confident that I can bring value in any room!

4. I am so happy with my life, living with the love of my life and our two kids. We live in a wonderful house close to downtown or on the water with no financial worries. I drive a blacked-out Range Rover and Rolls Royce. My wife drives whatever car she wants! My business runs on auto pilot and I make $10 million a year, working 10-20 hours per week. I travel with my family and friends at my leisure. My parents are happily retired in a house of their dreams. I truly love my life and my beautiful wife!

I have these affirmations taped to the mirror in my bathroom, on my dresser, on the dashboard of my cars, and on my phone so no matter what I am doing, I see them and think about them. I look in the mirror in the morning after brushing my teeth and stare at myself in the mirror and say these affirmations to myself every day. As you start to say these affirmations on a regular basis, you actually start to become the person that you are affirming you are. Your mind and body look for ways to make those things real.

Other examples of affirmations could be:

1. I accept what I cannot change.
2. I have control over my thoughts, feelings, and choices.
3. I know, accept, and am true to myself.
4. I learn from my mistakes.
5. I am the man/women I want my kids to look up to.

6. I am in a position where I can help my own family, siblings, and parents.

They can be anything that you want to live out!

You need to think about who you want to be and what you want to have confidence in. Write down affirmations that make you feel that way.

Stop reading now and write down those affirmations. Start saying them today!

Make copies of your affirmations and put them in places that you will see every day.

The other thing that I did was to create a vision board for myself to keep me motivated throughout the day. On my vision board I put down everything that I wanted: A Range Rover, Rolls Royce, box of nice watches, airplane to travel in, motorcycle, and many other things. I put a poster board on my wall with pictures of everything that I wanted in my life on it.

After repeating my affirmations every morning, I would visualize myself enjoying the things that were on my vision board. Close your eyes and see yourself driving that car you want, living in your dream house, taking a trip to your dream vacation spot. Think about what it feels like, what it looks like, how it tastes, who is with you. Tie in as many positive emotions to your vision as possible. These emotions and thoughts will keep you motivated when it seems everything is going against you.

About 1.5 years after I started doing these things, my business exploded. I went from working on single projects to managing multiple projects at a time. Instead of managing a few hundred thousand dollars at any given time, I was managing millions and millions of dollars in deals. My income has increased 4X in the last year and a half.

If you live in doubt and fear, your income and business can never outgrow you. Doubting yourself is hurting you more than you could ever imagine. Maybe there was an opportunity of a lifetime starring you in the face, but because you were scared or doubted your capabilities, you passed on the opportunity or maybe didn't even see it since you weren't ready for it. Get doubt and fear out of your head as soon as possible and opportunity will come in abundance. You need to be so confident in yourself and your skills that a negative thought never stays in your head for longer than a second.

I specifically remember an opportunity where I had to purchase a building in a neighborhood that I wasn't super familiar with. The purchase price of the building was $30,000 and the renovation was going to cost $300,000. That would have been the biggest project I would have done to date and I was nervous that I wouldn't be able to raise the money to purchase and renovate the building. More importantly, it was a bigger building than normal, so I needed a different type of contractor and I did not know any. So, I was scared I wouldn't find anyone to complete the project after I purchased it.

Due to my fears and doubts, I passed on the deal. Now, every day when I drive past that building, which is now worth over $600,000, I regret my decision. Buying that building would have been one of the best investments I could have made in my career and I missed my opportunity because of the fears of not raising money and not finding the right contractor. Now that I have seen what could have been, and the growth and confidence in myself, there is absolutely no chance I would pass on such an opportunity now. My unwavering confidence in myself means that I know I would be able to figure out how to make any deal work.

Although it was a hard lesson to learn, I have put the things in place which help motivate me to achieve my goals. Those things include learning from opportunities missed, my daily affirmations, and my vision board.

A lot of people struggle with self-confidence at times. It's okay, I did to! It is all about how you approach a situation now. If you have doubt and questions on how you are going to accomplish your next big goal, and you are thinking of all of the ways it might fail – Guess what, it is probably going to fail.

Even on business ventures or decisions I make where there is a large possibility of things failing and/or losing money, I don't ever think about the failure. I only think about the successes that could come from it. Everybody in life is going to fail at some point, you just have to get up, keep your confidence, and press on until your breakthrough comes!

Never let fear or lack of confidence in yourself allow you to miss out on the opportunity of a lifetime! You will live the rest of your life in regret if you do!

Your Action Steps

1. Write out 5 affirmations about the person you want to be and post them on the mirror in your bathroom, in your car,

on your fridge, anywhere where you see them and read them aloud to yourself every morning.

2. Create your vision board of all of the things/goals you want and post it in your bedroom or anywhere in your house where you see it multiple times per day, every day.

Chapter 9 – Only Worry About What You Can Control

I have grown up my entire life seeing what is "normal" and what everyone says is normal. But who determines what normal actually is? I think the only thing that is normal in this life is what you allow to be normal. Normal is what you accept and believe. I am a very avid believer that you can do anything in this life!

Is it normal to own a private jet? Absolutely not, but there's people who own one... some own a few.

Is it normal to be in the 1% and make millions of dollars? No, it's not, but there are plenty of people that make millions of dollars every single month.

Is it normal that people go on vacations for 30-60-90 days at a time or even travel their entire life? No, it's not, but some people still do it.

Normal is what you allow it to be. You have to ask yourself what you want your "normal" to be for your life and then go out and make it a reality. All of the things I have mentioned earlier in this book, visualizing your perfect day, saying your affirmations, creating a vision board, etc. are ways to define how you want your "normal" life to be like. Go out there and make those things a reality!

I remember when I was still working 60-80 hours per week, and making good money doing it, but I was working nonstop. I thought that it was normal. To make a lot of money, you have to work a lot of hours. However, one of my mentors drilled it into me that the amount of time you work and the amount of productivity you have in a day are not always equal. You can work for 15 hours but actually only be productive for four to five of those hours, wasting the rest of the day away on things you can't control.

Since then I have changed two things in my life that have saved me an insane amount of time and allow me to be much more productive, work less, and have more time to spend with the people that I love and doing the things that I want to do.

The first change I made in my life was that I decided to not worry about the things that I have zero control over. There are things in life that you can control, and you should spend time making sure those things are in order. Things like balancing your books, looking over accounts, what time you wake up, what you eat/drink, sending out marketing every week, and doing your weekly team meetings. But there are many things in business, and in life, that you have no control over. The more time you spend worrying about those things, the less time you have to focus on income producing activities and the less productive you will be.

For example, I went to dinner with my good friend Malon a few months ago and the valet parked my car. We had an awesome dinner, talked a lot about business and life, and as we were leaving, I had my car pulled around for me. When they pulled my car around, they drove past us and parked the car a few cars away which I thought was really weird. I looked at Malon and said, "I bet money they messed my car up." The valet got out of the car and started running towards us and said that my side window was kicked in, the door was dented, and seat cushions were ripped when the glass fell into the car. I started laughing since I had already figured that something had happened. I very calmly asked for my claim ticket back that I gave to them to retrieve the car and looked at the back of the ticket. The small print said, "We are not responsible for theft of any items left behind in vehicle or damage to vehicle we did not cause." I handed him back the ticket, said it was all good and got in the car and drove off.

On top of the damage to the car, two of my bags were stolen, one with some clothes and three pairs of shoes in, and my work bag, that had my laptop and journal in it. The items alone that were stolen totaled about $8,000 and with the damage to the vehicle the total claim being about $16,000 in total. All of which I couldn't control. My car getting broke into and things being stolen are all things that I could not control or change in any way, shape, or form. So why spend time worrying about how it happened, where my belongings were, or driving up and down through the neighborhood all night looking for someone carrying my backpack? It would be a complete waste of time.

Yes, I drove to where the car was parked to see if there were any cameras, and there weren't. I tracked my phone and laptop, yet they never came back online. Outside of that, I called my insurance company, opened a claim and sent in the details of the belongings that were stolen. I also took my car in to be fixed. After that, I let the insurance companies deal with it. That is why I have insurance. I went to the Apple store the next morning, bought another laptop and ordered everything else off of Amazon. In less than a day of dealing with all of this, I was right back on my path and journey to chase my dreams.

I didn't spend any time worrying about the situation or how I was going to pay for it or why it happened to me. I could not control the events leading up to the items being stolen or the events afterwards. I could have spent all week worrying about that and got nothing done while in the office and my brain would have been all over the place with no productivity.

Only spend time worrying about things that you have control over!

Let me give you another example: I went to purchase a house and I could not sleep all night worrying about the "what ifs".

- What if I overpaid for the house?
- What if some things go wrong?
- What if I don't sell it for what I need to sell it for to make money?

Yes, you can plan and cross your t's and dot your i's, but don't get stuck worrying about details that you can't control. I showed up to that house the next morning and sat there ALL day with the inspector. I could have been out using that time to look for another house to make even more money. But I decided to waste it spending time sitting there following an inspector around all day even though he could have sent me a 10-page report that evening with all of the findings. It would have been the same outcome, but would have taken only twenty minutes of my time as compared to the hours I actually spent at that house.

Once I got the report back later that night, I asked for a $15,000 reduction on the price from the seller as the house needed way more work than I had budgeted for. Again, I stayed up worrying about whether they were going to give me the reduction or not. Two days later, the seller got back to me and said no, they would not reduce the price and they terminated the contract. I had wasted an entire week worrying so much about this property and the "what-ifs" that I didn't do anything else all week. I didn't look for other houses, look for private lenders, or find contractors, nothing! I sat there and worried about a situation where no matter what I did, I could not have changed or swayed in any way.

After learning the hard way and wasting a ton of time on situations I couldn't control, I learned and now only spend my time on high income producing activities that I can control and strategize about. I don't waste time worrying about things I can't control.

Worrying about the uncontrollable is a waste of time, so stop doing it!

The second change that I made in my life was taking all the negativity out of my life. If you tolerate negative things and negative people, then that becomes the normal in your life. I don't accept that.

Anything negative in my life was removed. Negative people, negative situations, even things in my house that brought back a negative memory were removed. Sometimes negative thoughts are going to pop into your head, but you have the luxury of choosing what to do with those negative thoughts. You can give into them, pump them up, and make them bigger than they are, or you can IMMEDIATELY eliminate that negative thought or situation from your life. Now, as soon as a negative thought comes into my mind, it is eliminated.

I am sure everyone has had situations in their life where they make a problem way bigger than it needs to be and then end up finding out that they have blown the situation way out of proportion and wasted an immense amount of time.

There was a time in my business where finances were not where they needed to be. My cash flow was really poor, and I was worrying about how to make payroll one month. I had used my money to fund overages on project budgets and to purchase other plots of land and houses to put in inventory for future projects. The payroll was due as was a $75,000 credit card payment.

I sat at my desk one night after the team left and I put together a spreadsheet of where all of my money was. I listed what deals I had lent money out on, what overages on construction I had paid out of pocket, what money I had in projects that were in inventory, and all of the upcoming expenses I could foresee for the next month. I owed way more money in the next 30 days then I had coming in. I had stretched myself too thin this time.

I spent nearly two hours that night putting together the spreadsheet and stressed over it every night. Every day after work

I opened that spreadsheet and reviewed it as those payments came closer to being due. I got more and more nervous and thinking, "Man, what am I going to do? I'm not going to have the money to pay these people." I robbed time from my team and my life that I could have been looking for more deals or training them better in their position. After two weeks of worrying about this, and thinking negatively about the outcome, I realized what I was doing and removed all negative thought. I concluded there were two options. One being that some of the houses would actually close on time for invoices to be paid.

The second option was to pick up the phone and call some of my lenders, show them my spreadsheet to prove that although I had all of the money, my cash flow and reserves was poor at the moment. I would borrow the money from them but would have to pay them a substantial amount in interest for lending me the money. I took all the negative thoughts out of my head and decided that either way, it was all going to work out and that my life and business would continue keeping on no matter what.

Then guess what? We sold a house a couple days before the money was due and I had more than enough money to pay the bills at that point. Would that have happened if I kept thinking negatively? Maybe, but what I do know for sure is that once I removed the worry and negativity from my mind, my brain was freed up to go out there and get back to business, and I could focus on other incoming producing activities like looking for houses that would move my business forward, not backwards.

You will stay in the same rut that you are in right now if you continue to think negatively about a situation. Remove that negativity from your life and you will have way more time. You'll sleep better and will be happier every day!

This chapter is about being conscious of how you spend your time. There are only 24 hours in a day. Even the wealthiest people in the world still only have 24 hours in each day. They can't buy more time. The difference between us and them is that they are so insanely productive with their time that they just get more done in a day then we do with the same amount of time.

Time is literally the only thing in this world that you can never get more of. You can't create it or buy it. Once it is gone, it is gone for good and you will never get it back!

If you were to work 40 hours per week, 52 weeks of the year, you would work 2,080 hours. Think about how much money you want to make in a year and write that number down. Let's say you want to make $100,000 in a year. If you divide $100,000 by the total number of work hours available of 2080, your time would be valued at $48.08 per hour ($100,000/2080).

If your time is valued at $48.08 per hour, do you think it is a good use of your time to spend a day thinking negatively about a situation that, no matter what you do, you have zero control over?

If you spent an hour worrying and thinking negatively then you just lost $48.08. If you spend a day worrying about it, you lose $384.64 based on an eight-hour workday.

What if you have bigger goals?

If you want to make $1,000,000 in a year, and divide that by 2080 hours, your time would be valued at $480.77 per hour.

If your time is now valued at $480.77 per hour, do you think it is a good use of your time to spend a day thinking negatively about a situation that, no matter what you do, you have zero control over?

For every hour you spend worrying and thinking negatively, you just lost $480.77. If you spend a day worrying about it, you just lost $3,846.16 based on an eight-hour workday.

When you realize the value of time, you won't want to waste any of it!

Knowing that, I am now super conscious of how I spend my time, who I spend it with and the thoughts I allow in my head. I try not to waste any time whatsoever in any aspect of my life. My family laughs at me sometimes if I try to save one-minute driving home and catching a light vs. waiting in traffic or missing a light.

There are however a couple of things you need to note.

- At the beginning of any business, you need to work your face off and do anything and everything necessary to achieve your dreams. You don't really have the luxury of paying people to do things for you. You can control the worry and negative thinking in your head, but you still have to work hard!

- Don't get so strict with your time that you don't have time to enjoy the people and things around you. Remember how I said that thinking properly about time, worry, and removing negativity actually allows you to be more productive. This then allows you to spend more time with the people that you love.

Don't allow worry and negative thinking to hold you back from achieving your goals. Determine now that you are going to remove all negative thoughts from your thinking and only worry about things that you can control. Then, and only then, will you be well on your way to achieving your dreams!

Your Action Steps

1. Allow no negativity in your life.
   - Add an affirmation to your daily routine of, "I will only think positively, and I will not allow any negativity into my life"
2. Do the time calculation of how valuable your time is so you are conscious of your value and don't waste any more time.
   - Amount of money you want to make in a year in dollars divided by 2,080 = hourly value.

Chapter 10 – The Abundance Mentality

There are trillions of dollars on this planet and billions of dollars moving every single day. There is no shortage of anything in this world. If you fly down to the Caribbean and look around, there are thousands of private jets and private yachts sitting around. Many of which cost hundreds of millions of dollars.

I am currently writing this book in Anguilla. This island is only 37 square miles and there are at least 20 private jets at the airport! I also saw some huge yachts down on the beaches. I even saw a small boat leave from the shore, go to one of those yachts taking the passengers back to the boat, and they parked their boat inside of the yacht. Hit a button, a garage door type thing opens, and they just drive the small boat into the yacht, closing the door behind them. There is no shortage of money out here!

During the first half of my career, I got caught up into the scarcity mindset. When I got into real estate, I was sat in a room with hundreds of other people all trying to get into real estate. I was thinking, "How is there going to be enough deals out there for all of us to make money?" I saw everything as competition and thought only about how I could get the few deals out there and make some money instead of them getting those deals.

Every lead I got I squeezed it so tightly and tried to squeeze every little piece of profit out of it that I could. I was so stuck on every individual lead or deal that I am sure I missed tons of other opportunities because my sights were so narrow.

When I finally learned about the abundance mentality, my life changed forever. Instead of thinking about how to make every little lead work, I knew in my head that there was plenty of opportunity out there for everyone to make money in this business. I started opening up to my competitors and talking with them about their business and their deals and how we could work together to make some money. Deals started to flow in like never before!

When I mentioned earlier that my business went from single to multiple deals at any time, part of that transition was thinking more abundantly. When you are willing to walk away from an opportunity because it doesn't make sense instead of forcing something to be that truly isn't, then you are in the abundance mindset. However, if you sit there for days trying to figure out how to make something work that simply does not work, then you are still in the scarcity mindset.

Start thinking in abundance and opportunity will flow into you!

When I started thinking in abundance, I started to partner/joint venture on deals with others which meant more money and more opportunities coming in. Now, at any time, I have five to ten joint ventures going on which has turned into an entirely new income stream for me. This would never have been there if I continued to penny pinch every opportunity I had.

I used to keep all of my secrets and thoughts to myself and that kept me small. Now that I think in abundance, I know there is plenty of opportunity out there and I want to do deals with others. Without opening up into abundance, I would never be able to do JV deals with others and have another stream of income.

Obtaining that abundance mentality is not an easy thing to do. It took me years to truly believe in abundance, and even to this day, there are times where I struggle to think abundantly. Things start to go bad, you start to worry and become scared about losing deals and opportunities. But like I have said before, whatever you think in your mind becomes your reality!

A few months ago, we had a lot of deals in motion and money moving and I started to worry about money. I started to think scarce and how things weren't going how they were supposed to go and closings were getting delayed and I was worrying about how I was going to pay payroll. At the end of the month, I looked at the board and we made over $200K that month, which was one of our best months.

However, those scarce thoughts became a trickle effect. The month after that we had one of our worst months. This is because I took my thoughts from abundance to scarcity and the following month was terrible because of that. When the scarce thoughts were there, I picked up on my thought process and removed it and went back to abundance mentality. The month after that, we made over $200K again.

If I start thinking scarce and think about the few deals that are out there then that becomes true. Yet, if I continually know that there is abundance everywhere, then my brain will look and find opportunities in everyday activities and I experience abundance!

To stay in abundance, you need to consciously think abundantly every single day. Don't ever let negativity or thoughts of scarcity into your head!

Your Action Steps

1. Add this affirmation to your list:

   "I know there is always an abundance of opportunity in this world and I will never let scarcity thoughts into my mind."

2. Give to people so it will come full circle. The more you give, the more you get. When you are tight with information, people don't reach out to you as much for advice or business opportunities. If you give value and knowledge, those same people will be the ones who bring the opportunities back to you to participate in.

Chapter 11 – It's All Worth It

Will all of the things mentioned in this book happen overnight? No!

You may have been thinking negatively for years, have surrounded yourself with the wrong people, and maybe you don't have the best work ethic.

I was in that position less than 5 years ago!

It has taken me years of working towards my goals to change my mindset and thought process. I am nowhere near perfect and continue to work on my mindset every single day. It is a never-ending challenge to continue bettering yourself.

If you want to achieve your dreams and design your own lifestyle, you need to start right now. You need to start today. Hence why there are Action Steps at the end of each chapter in this book. I have read hundreds of books and put in countless hours figuring out how to change my mindset and this book is the key takeaways from the lessons that I have learned over the past five years.

I love the grind, I love the chase, and I love winning so my journey of learning will never end! I will always be trying to better myself by seeking mentors, working on my mindset, and working every single day to achieve the goals, dreams, and lifestyle that I want for myself and my family.

I posted a picture on Instagram this morning of my laptop out on a sun lounger by the pool at the back of the 4-bedroom Villa in Anguilla where I am vacationing for thirty days. The picture had the quote, "Right back to it. Even on vacation, work doesn't stop."

One of my close friends and mentors, Terry Thayer, responded to my post and said, "It's not work when you enjoy it and you do it on your terms where you want." I could not agree more!

You chase your goals and do the hard work so you can live a lifestyle that you want to live. I love what I do in real estate and will always do real estate, but that does not mean that I have to be on the ground working in the houses every single day. I grinded for almost 5 years straight, put the hard work in, and took the risks that allow me to now travel and do the things that I want to do.

It has always been a dream of mine to take a 3-month trip away from everything and just island hop down in the Caribbean or go to Europe and see the world outside of what I am used to and what is considered "normal". Going on a 3-month vacation is definitely not normal, but I am making it the normal in my own life. While on this trip, people have looked at me like I was crazy when I tell them I am in the middle of a 3-month vacation and they always ask, "How are you doing that?"

This trip goes against what people are used to and what is normal for them. I don't ever let other people's opinions shape my life and my dreams. You can never let anyone's opinion change your goals and dreams. Even before leaving for this trip, I would tell people what I was going to do and they would look at me and ask how I was doing it: How the business would run without me being there?

The trip lasted for thirty days as I wanted to get back as I am still building a business where I can vacation not just for 3 months but for a lifetime!

I often think back to when I was lost and confused and didn't know what to do with my life. That was less than five years ago! Back then I had just moved back to Columbus, I was no longer playing basketball, which had been my entire life for over eight years, and I was living with my parents. I still remember the days where I was working over 100 hours a week, running myself ragged, and I was broke and not sleeping much.

I remember feeling like I was a failure but knowing that there was so much more in store in my life and at one point literally crawling under my parents dining room table and bawling my eyes out because I was stuck and had an opportunity that I was about to miss. I remember the nervousness I had after swiping my credit card and maxing out my card of $10K+, and for the next 16 months grinding my face off every day and not making a single penny chasing my dreams. I remember my friends stopped inviting me to do things because they said I always told them no when they did because I had bigger visions and working in my parent's basement writing letters and stuffing envelopes getting paper cuts every week until two, three, even four o'clock in the morning at times.

I remember all of the struggle, the hurt, the loneliness, the scarcity mindset, the times away from the people I loved, the long hours put in, and the unknown of ever making it.

Through all of that, I focused on building myself and building my own mentality and thought process and being so confident in myself even when people around me were trying to tear me down. I surrounded myself with people that continued to motivate me and encourage me to chase my goals. I unfollowed everyone on social media that didn't add value to my life and also anyone who was negative. I followed people on social media that had similar goals and visions that I did and people that were always positive and always motivating.

But after all of that, what I remember most now is the feelings I had when I sold my first house and got a check in my hand for $184K, (this was not all profit, actual net profit was $103K). I remember making enough money where I could take trips when I wanted to and being able to buy the things I wanted to buy for my mom, dad, sister, grandma, and myself. I remember flying my parents down to Saint Martin for a week and staying in a 4 bedroom villa with crazy views and spending time with them. I will always remember sitting on the balcony of the villa I am staying at while on this vacation and obtaining another goal/dream of mine: writing this book!

I don't say all of this to brag. I say this so when you are on your journey and you face the same obstacles and heartaches that I did, that you know what to look forward to! Doing something to change your life is not going to be smooth sailing.

Was it all worth it? Absolutely without a doubt!

That dark place you are in now doesn't have to last forever. Find your passion from your journaling, take that leap of faith by meeting and networking with others, and grind every day until your break comes and you can live the life you want to live! Don't let negativity or anything else hold you back from your dreams!

Follow me on Instagram @AustinRutherfordOfficial or on Facebook at "Austin Rutherford". I am on there every day talking about the daily grind and providing motivation on how to help you chase your goals and how to deal with the struggles you will run in to.

Tag me on IG when you take your leap of faith, I would love to see your progress and growth along the way!!

Go to www.FlippingTheRightWay.com to sign up for my email list. This list will add value to your life and includes real world experiences and struggles to get you over the cliff, to encourage you to make that jump, and to keep you motivated through the grind every single day!

I look forward to connecting with you and adding value any way that I can!

Just a kid from Columbus,
    Austin Rutherford

Made in the USA
Middletown, DE
20 June 2019